PLAYS FOR SMALL STAGES

PLAYS
FOR SMALL STAGES

BY

MARY ALDIS

Mrs. Pat and the Law—The Drama Class
Extreme Unction — The Letter
Temperament

One-Act Play Reprint Series

Core Collection Books, inc.
GREAT NECK, NEW YORK

First Published 1915
Reprinted 1976

International Standard Book Number
0-8486-2000-3

Library of Congress Catalog Number
76-40384

PRINTED IN THE UNITED STATES OF AMERICA

TO
MY BOYS

NOTE

The author desires to express gratitude for assistance in the preparation and presentation of these plays to Mr. and Mrs. Charles Atkinson, Mr. Benjamin Carpenter, Mr. Arthur Davison Ficke, Mr. Hobart Chatfield-Taylor, and many others of that sympathetic group of players, authors, and audiences who have together made The Playhouse possible.

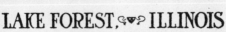

CONTENTS

PREFACE

No one can deny the present Dramatic Renaissance. Plays profitable and unprofitable, popular and unpopular, proper and improper, plays priggish and plays profane, are being presented, read, discussed, revised, written about and quarrelled over. The Drama is furiously to the fore and, in spite of the "Movies," continues to hold the absorbed interest of an increasing number of people.

In the midst of all this dramatic stir, this unrest of expression, certain ones, weary of being onlookers, arise and announce, "We too will act," and others cry out, "We too will write." So the Amateur providing his own cue, makes his entrance, and after being regarded a bit askance by "The Profession" is allowed to play his part.

In the Spring of 1911 I cast an affectionate and calculating eye upon a small frame house next door. It was shortly acquired; partitions and ceilings were pulled out, the lean-to kitchen became the stage; dressing-rooms were added and a miniature theatre which we called The Playhouse was ready.

In the five Summers since, a group of amateur players have presented some fifty one-act plays to the great pleasure and interest of themselves and the alternate, sometimes mingled, amusement, surprise, disapproval and horror of their neighbors.

Many of the plays given were written by the players themselves or adapted from short stories. Others were translated from the French, German or Italian. All were experimental, undertaken in a spirit of adventure with the simple motive of amusing the players and their friends. The five plays in this book were written for production at "The Playhouse." They have all gained in rehearsal by suggestions from the actors. In the comedies much is left to the interpretation of the players. Often amusing lines or "business" comes to a player from the response of the audience, but he and his fellows must be quick of wit that such improvisation may seem entirely natural.

Amateurs have one great advantage, they give a play only once or twice and so attain a freshness and spontaneity that it would take years of technical training to enable them to keep up through a long run. H. T. Parker, commenting in *The Boston Transcript* upon a performance of the "Lake Forest Players" on a dramatic visit to the Toy Theatre in Boston says:

" Time and again amateurs attain simplicity because they do not suspect intricacy, and truth because they see it and embody it in their acting with no veils of habit, method or precedent. Given histrionic instinct, aptitude and observation, they act with ease, freedom and variety, and with full self-surrender to their parts. If the means are not the professional means they do their office which is to bring the personages to life in the terms of the play. Acting for themselves and in their own way, they are not weighted with self-consciousness, tradition or imitative effort."

The word self-consciousness is the key-note. "Drop self-consciousness and get under the skin of the character you portray" might be considered the theory of amateur acting.

Occasionally efforts have been made at The Playhouse to select a stage director, but as each participant takes advice and direction in inverse ratio to the firmness with which he is able to maintain his own views the plan has not proved effective. Our composite results are obtained by a process of mutual suggestion and recrimination, and if these simple means fail it is never from any shyness on the part of a fellow-actor in expressing an honest opinion.

There are two rules posted in the Green Room:

KEEP YOUR TEMPER

AND

RETURN YOUR MANUSCRIPTS.

The second is imperative, the first variable in application.

In selecting plays we have departed radically from the amateur tradition of resuscitating "plays with a punch," which have fared well in the hands of professionals. In the established "tricks of the trade" of course the amateur cannot compete with the professional. This is the true significance of the well-known Green Room hoot that "The worst professional is better than the best amateur."

We generally try to give our audiences something they have not heard before, and seek plays in which the expressed word, the mental attitude and the interplay of character are of more importance than the physical action. Here, if anywhere, although such plays may seem difficult, lies the amateur's opportunity. So we are not afraid of plays with little action and much talk, for is not the most intense drama of all, the drama of the soul, the struggle between mind and mind, heart and heart? There lies all the pain, the joy, the perplexity of life. It is in talk, low and intense, gay and railing, bitter and despairing, as the case may be, that we moderns carry on our drama of life, the foundation for the drama of the stage.

MARY ALDIS.

Lake Forest, Illinois.
July, 1915.

MRS. PAT AND THE LAW

Played for the first time on September 14, 1913, by Mr. BENJAMIN CARPENTER, Mrs. ARTHUR ALDIS, Miss POLLY CHASE, Miss ISABEL McBIRNEY, *and* Mr. CHAS. ATKINSON.

MRS. PAT AND THE LAW.

CHARACTERS:

    PATRICK O'FLAHERTY.

    NORA O'FLAHERTY, *his wife.*

    JIMMIE, *his crippled son, aged about eight or ten years.*

    MISS CARROLL, *the Visiting Nurse.*

    JOHN BING, *a Policeman.*

SCENE: *A small, poor room in a tenement flat. Cook-stove, back; shabby lounge, front; at left, kitchen table with a faded flower in a bottle; a wash-tub on bench, centre left, back near door. At left, door to bedroom. At right, door to hallway.*

When the curtain rises NORA O'FLAHERTY *is discovered at the wash-tub. She is a large woman, with a worn, sweet face, across her forehead an ugly red cut. The room is untidy, and so is* NORA. *The stove is blazing hot. After stirring the clothes in the boiler* NORA *wipes her face with the back of her hand and sighs wearily as she puts a fresh lot into the tub of suds.*

JIMMIE.

[*Speaking from bedroom.*]

Maw, what time is it?

NORA.

Most tin, Jimmie-boy.

JIMMIE.

Whin 'll Miss Carroll come?

NORA.

Well, now, I shouldn't wonder if she'd be comin' along the shtreet and oup the shtairs and right in at that door about the time the clock gits 'round to half past tin, or maybe it's sooner she'll be. Do you think it's a flower she'll be bringin' today, Jimmie-boy?

JIMMIE.

To-day's Tuesday, ain't it?

NORA.

Shure!

JIMMIE.

There's no tellin'. Sometimes she says there ain't enough to go 'round.
[*A pause.*]

NORA.

[*Sorting out clothes.*]
Sakes alive—the wash that's on me! I'll niver git through.
[*A short silence.*]

JIMMIE.

Maw, what time is it now?

NORA.

Well, I couldn't rightly say, the steam bein' in me eyes like. Faith, ye must bear in mind there's many that's needin' her.

Maybe at this very minute it's a new-born baby just come into the world she's tendin', or an ould man just goin' out of it! She'll be comin' soon now, I'll warrant ye.

JIMMIE.

But, Maw, me leg hurts, and Paw takes all the room in the bed, he's sleepin' so noisy!

NORA.

Och, Jimmie darlin', have a little patience! Me name's not Nora O'Flaherty if Miss Carroll don't bring us a flower this day, or if there ain't enough to go 'round, shure it's the bright happy worrd or the little joke or plan she'll have in her mind for ye 'ull hearten the day as well as a flower.

[*Another pause.*]

JIMMIE.

Maw! Ain't it half past tin yit?

NORA.

Oh, laddie, an' I hadn't the great wash on me hands I'd dance a jig t' amuse ye! Shure many's the song I've sung an' the jig I've danced whin I was a slip o' a gurrl back in the ould counthree, afore I had the four of yiz and yer Paw to look afther! Now it's me arrms have need to move livelier than me legs, I'm thinkin'. Listen, now, an' I'll see if I can call to mind a little song for ye. [*Sings, keeping time with the wash-board.*]

> There was a lady lived at Rhin,
> A lady very stylish, man—

But she snapped her fingers at all her kin
 And—she fell in love wid an Irishman.
 A wild tremenjous Irishman,
 A rampin', stampin' Irishman,
 A devil-may-take-'em—Bad as you make 'em—
 Fascinatin' Irishman!

Oh, wan o' his een was bottle green
 And the tother wan was out, me dear,
 An' the calves o' his wicked twinklin' legs
 Were two feet 'round about, me dear.
 Oh—the slashin', dashin' Irishman—
 The blatherin', scatherin' Irishman,
 A whiskey, frisky, rummy, gummy,
 Brandy, dandy Irishman!

An' that was the lad the lady loved
 Like all the gurrls o' quality.
 He'd smash all the skulls o' the men o' Rhin
 Just by the way o' jollity.
 Oh, the ratlin', battlin' Irishman!
 The thumpin', bumpin' Irishman,
 The great he-rogue, wid his roarin' brogue!
 The laughin', quaffin' Irishman!*

There's a song fer ye now! Ha, Jimmie-boy, I'm thinkin'
that song 'u'd had more sense an' it told what she did wid her
rampin', roarin' Irishman wanst she got married to him.

[*Knock on the hall door.*]

JIMMIE.

Ah, that's her!

NORA.

There! Didn't I tell ye? [NORA *wipes her hands and hurries
to open the door, admitting* MISS CARROLL.] Ah! Miss Carroll

* A‹ter Wm. McGinn.

dear, it's welcome ye are this day. Jimmie's been watchin'
and wearyin' for ye since the daylight dawned. How are ye?
[She has turned away as MISS CARROLL *enters so as to conceal
her head, but* MISS CARROLL *catches sight of it and,
taking hold of her arm, turns her around.]*

MISS CARROLL.

Why, Mrs. O'Flaherty, what an awful cut! You look as if
you had been hit with an axe!

NORA.

Oh, git along with ye!

MISS CARROLL.

How did it happen?

NORA.

Shure, 'twas nothin' at all but his boot, and he that unstiddy
he couldn't aim shtraight! It's 'most well now. *[She turns to
tub.]*

MISS CARROLL.

[Taking off her coat and opening her satchel.]
It isn't "'most well." It's a fresh wound and a bad, deep cut.
As I've told you before, I've no patience with you for putting
up with such treatment. Don't you know the law would protect you? You ought to swear out a warrant for your husband's
arrest on the grounds of personal violence. That might teach
him a lesson. This is the third time now in a month he's struck
you. It's outrageous! Has he got a job yet?

JIMMIE.

Ain't you comin', Miss Carroll? Me leg hurts awful.

MISS CARROLL.

Yes, Jimmie-boy, in a minute. [*She has been getting hot water from the stove, preparing cotton gauze, etc., for dressing. She stops a moment in her work and regards* MRS. O'FLAHERTY.] Has he got a job yet?

NORA.

He had work last week.

MISS CARROLL.

For how long?

NORA.

For three days—an' a part o' four.

MISS CARROLL.

And then he got drunk and got turned off, eh? And you gave him your wash money, too, I suppose, as usual.

NORA.

No, no, Miss Carroll dear, I didn't do that at all. I only give him the half of it, and niver any of it would he have had but— well—knowin' it was in the house, it was coaxin' me mornin' and night he was with that wheedlin', soft way o' him, and the silly loverin' talk till the heart just ran melty within me. [MISS

CARROLL *regards her with he. lips pursed.*] I know it's an ould fool you're thinkin' me, but jest let you be listenin' to his talk wanst and see what you'd do, and him tellin' stories to Jimmie the while so kind and lovely.

MISS CARROLL.

[Stopping at entrance to bedroom, basin in hand.]

"Kind and lovely" indeed! When he takes your wages and hurts and abuses you, and Jimmie hasn't a decent place to live in because his father's a lazy— *[She stops in amazement on the threshold as she sees* PAT *asleep in the room within.]* Well, I never! *[Comes back into the room.]* Mrs. O'Flaherty, you must make Pat get up and get out of there while I take care of Jimmie.

*[*MRS. O'FLAHERTY *looks injured, but wipes her hands and does as she is bid.* MISS CARROLL *stands watching at the door.]*

NORA.

[Within bedroom.]

Pat! Pat! Wake up, will ye! *[*PAT *groans.]* My, but you're sleepin' hard! Pat! Miss Carroll says ye're to git oup and git out o' here while she takes care o' Jimmie. Come along, now! That's right, Jimmie-boy, give him a good thump! Are ye oup on yer legs now? Mind what yer doin'. There ye are!

PAT.

[Entering, yawning.]

Wha' for Miss Carroll says git oup and git out?

*[*MISS CARROLL *glares at* PAT. PAT, *turning, catches her eye and smiles sweetly ere she vanishes into the bedroom.]*

Nora.

Well, Pat O'Flaherty, I'm thinkin' Miss Carroll ain't so awful admirin' o' your ways! Sometimes I'm thinkin' she sees 'em clearer nor your lovin' wife does!

[Pat *picks up one of his shoes, sits down on the sofa and looks around for the other; pays no heed to* Nora's *talk.*]

Pat.

Where's me other shoe? [*Gets down on hands and knees and looks under the sofa.*] Shure I had the two of 'em on me feet yesterday. [*Laughs gaily.*] Maybe I wore wan on 'em out lookin' for that job that I didn't git!

[Nora *watches him a moment, then hands him the shoe she has picked up near the stove.*]

Nora.

Here's your shoe.

Pat.

Ah! That's the darlin'; thank ye kindly. I'd be losin' me head some day if 'twern't for you, Nora gurrl.

Nora.

[*At tub while* Pat *slowly puts on shoes.*]

Oh, Pat, ye will thry and git some worrk today, won't ye, man? Thry harrd. If they don't take ye on at the first place, go on an' don't git discouraged. Ye know ye're the grand workman whin ye thry, and ye must git a stiddy job soon. Ye really must, Pat. I'm shtrong; I don't mind the washin' fer

me own sake. I'd do anythin' fer you and the childer, but whin
Jimmie frets at me to play with him, an' the others come rushin'
in from school a-wantin' thur maw to do this and that fer 'em,
shure it comes harrd an' I dassn't take me arrms from the
suds to 'tend on 'em and comfort 'em and cook 'em thur meals
nice like that visitin' housekeepin' lady told me to.

[PAT *has not been listening very attentively, but has taken
in the drift of* NORA'S *plea.*]

PAT.

[*Pulling himself together and putting on hat and coat.*]

Ah, Nora gurrl, I'll be gettin' a good job today shure. [*Suddenly catches sight of her forehead.*] Wha's that on your head?

NORA.

[*Startled.*]

Me head, is it? Miss Carroll was sayin' just now it was
"personal violence and breakin' the law." I was thinkin' afore
that 'twas only the heel o' an ould boot walked around daytimes
on Pat O'Flaherty, lookin' for a job.

[PAT *regards her uneasily, meditating speech, but appreciates he is too befuddled for argument, so begins to whistle
as he gets himself out and down-stairs, leaving the door
open.* NORA *goes to shut it, and stands a moment reflecting,
looking after* PAT, *then returns to the tub near the bedroom
door, evidently thinking. Short pause.*]

JIMMIE.

[*Within bedroom.*]

Say, Miss Carroll, d'ye think I'll ever git it?

Miss Carroll.

Christmas is coming, Jimmie-boy.

Jimmie.

Huh! So's Fourth o' July.

Miss Carroll.

We'll see what we can do.

Jimmie.

The other lady you told about me brung me a suit, but some cove lots bigger 'n me wore it all out first. I don' like it. Gee! but I wisht I had a bran'-new suit just wanst.
[Nora *makes a little yearning gesture towards the room.*]

Miss Carroll.

Now, Jimmie-boy, come along. It won't hurt much. When you're all fixed up on the lounge in there I've got something pretty for you.

Jimmie.

Another flower? What kind is it?

Miss Carroll.

We'll see. Now lean on me.
[*They enter.*]

Nora.

That's the lad. Are ye all fixed up now? He's gettin' lots better, ain't he, Miss Carroll?

[JIMMIE *is a pale, emaciated child with a wan little face of great sweetness of expression. His clothes are much too large for him. He holds up one bandaged leg and hobbles on crutches.* MISS CARROLL *helps him onto the lounge, produces from a paper by her satchel two pink roses, holding them up.*]

JIMMIE.

Gee! ain't they pretty! Can I keep 'em both?

MISS CARROLL.

Both for you, Jimmie-boy, and we'll see what can be done about the suit. Perhaps we can find one somewhere that's bran' new. [*She gets a book from the shelf.*] See if you can learn all the new words on this page before I come tomorrow, will you? That's a dear old boy! Now, Mrs. O'Flaherty, let's see about that forehead. Sit down here. [MISS CARROLL *places a chair, front stage.*]

NORA.

[*Washing.*]

Oh, what's the use botherin' about me head? It 'll git well of itself. It always does. Don't be mindin' me.

MISS CARROLL.

But, Mrs. O'Flaherty, you really must let me see to it. It's a bad cut.

NORA.

[*Wiping her hands.*]

Oh well, you're so good to Jimmie I'll have to oblige you. I suppose you haven't had many persons with holes in their heads made by boots to tind to?   But you're young, Miss Carroll dear, you're young yit. [*She seats herself with a sigh.*] I'm talkin' silly, Miss Carroll, but there's no room for a joke in me heart this day. I've been thinkin'—about what you said afore you wint in to Jimmie.

Miss Carroll.

[*Binding up the injured head.*]

Yes?

Nora.

You were tellin' me to git out a warrant 'gainst Pat.   Do you think it would keep him from drinkin' just for a bit till we git caught up on the rint and the furniture?   Do you think it would?

Miss Carroll.

Mrs. O'Flaherty, you know it's a shame and an outrage the way Pat's behaving.   He's wearing you out.   He'll do you harm some day and then what will become of Jimmie?   He ought to be taught a good lesson.

Nora.

Would they do any hurt to him, do you think, an' they locked him up?   Would they care for him kindly, and he maybe helpless like?

Miss Carroll.

They certainly would care for him.   Now, Mrs. O'Flaherty, you go over to the Maxwell Street Station and show them your forehead, and say you want Pat "took up" for a day or so just for a lesson, do you understand?

NORA.

Yes, I understand. Oh, it seems an awful thing to be doin'
to your own man, don't it? After all them things I said when
we got married? No, no, I niver could do it, niver! [*Goes
back to tub.*]

MISS CARROLL.

Well, then, tell Pat you may do it, anyway. It will make him
respect you. But you're such a softy, of course you'll do
nothing. I must go now. Mrs. Flaherty, you must not let
Pat sleep with Jimmie. It is not good for him.

NORA.

[*While* MISS CARROLL *is packing satchel and getting on bonnet
and coat.*]

Shure now, Miss Carroll, you're down on Pat for everythin'.
He's a good, lovin' paw to Jimmie-boy he is—makin' him happy
and pleasin' him like nobody else can. Everybody's kind to
Jimmie and nobody's kind to Pat—and they're just alike—
two childer they are—both on 'em foolish and lovin' and helpless
like, and I love 'em both. Oh, I love 'em! If you'd hear 'em
together an' you wid your eyes shut, it's hard set you'd be to say
which was the man and which was the child. Sometimes
I can't 'tind to me washin' fer listenin' to the funny talk o'
the two o' them. Wan time they'll be settin' on the high moon
for a throne, with the little shtars to wait on 'em and shootin'-
shtars to run errands; another, they'll be swimmin' along
through the deep green sea, a-passin' the time o' day an' makin'
little jokes to the fishes. Ah, ye ought to hear 'em go on!

Miss Carroll.

Well, I'm glad he amuses Jimmie when he's at home, but he ought to be at work, a great strong man like him! He needs a good lesson, Pat does. Good-bye, Jimmie-boy. Be sure and have the new words learned. [*She gives him a little pat, and with a wave of the hand goes out.* Nora *is unheeding* Jimmie's *call of* "*Maw.*" Jimmie *has not listened to the conversation between* Nora *and* Miss Carroll.]

Jimmie.

[*Raising himself and looking around.*]

Maw! She said she'd try and git me a bran'-new suit. Say, Maw, d'ye think she'll pay out her money fer it? I don't want her to do that. She just gets wages same as Paw. She told me how it was. Say, Maw, why don't Paw bring home no more wages?

Nora.

[*Coming to him, then taking sudden decision.*]

Jimmie-boy, Maw's goin' out. [*Hastily gets out a very queer bonnet and mantle while she speaks and arrays herself, putting bonnet on crooked to partially conceal bandage.*] You just lie quiet there like a good boy, an' a lamb's tail couldn't whisk itself three times till I'll be back again. I'm not goin' to be a fool softy no longer, and Paw'll bring home some more wages afther that lesson he's needin'. Are ye all right now? Ye won't be needin' anything? [*Pats him on the head, then leans over and kisses him fiercely, protectingly.*]

Jimmie.

Where you goin'?

NORA.

I'm goin' to git the law to help us if it can. [*She goes out and bangs the door.*]

[JIMMIE, *left alone, is very bored and listless. He turns over the book, then lets it fall, twists himself wearily. Suddenly his whole face brightens happily at a step outside. PAT'S gay whistle is heard coming up-stairs.*]

PAT.

[*Entering.*]

Hi, Jimmie-boy! There's the great lad for ye! All shtuffed full and a-runnin' over he is wid fine learnin' out of books. Did ye ever see the loike o' him? Sittin' up dressed like folks! Faith, it's the proud Pat I am this day! Let's see what great thing about the wide worrld is a-hidin' itself inside o' this yere. [*Picks up book.*]

JIMMIE.

I'm tired o' that. Tell me a story.

PAT.

A shtory, is it? An' me to be sittin' here tellin' a young lad shtories at the high noon of the day, and the job takin' itself wings to fly off, I might be catchin' and holdin' down and I to go afther it instid! [*Sitting down by JIMMIE.*] Where's your Maw?

JIMMIE.

I dunno. She said she wasn't going to be no fool softy no more, and then she went out quick like. What's a fool softy?

[PAT *is very uneasy. He does not answer, then goes to the door, looks out, comes back slowly.*]

JIMMIE.

Paw, me leg hurts awful today.   Tell me a story.

PAT.

All right, lad, I'll tell ye a story.   [*Sits down near sofa.*]   Did I ever tell you about the king of Ireland and his siven sons? No?   Once upon a time there was a great, high-up, noble king reigned over Ireland with a golden crown on his noble head an' a rulin' shtick in his hand—   Whin 'll your Maw be back?

JIMMIE.

I dunno.   Go on with the story.

PAT.

Well, this grand king had siven sons, all fair and beautiful they were in armour of silver and shteel, an' on their heads helmets covered with precious stones dug up out o' the earth that would make your eyes blink for the shinin'.   Bye-and-bye the siven lads grew up strong and mighty, and whin the king saw that they were gettin' to man's eshtate he got him together all of the workmen out of a job there were in the kingdom of Ireland, and he sets 'em to buildin' siven great castles, each wan on a different high-up mountain-top, so high that the peaks and shpires of some of them made holes right through the blue sky, do ye mind?   Well, whin the castles were all grand and ready he called his siven sons together, an' he stood 'em all up in a glitterin' row and he said to 'em, "Now, me byes, it's no end of a foine time ye've been havin' a-skylarkin' 'round me kingdom, but it's siven high castles I've built for ye now and ye'd better be gettin' yourselves wives and some bits of furniture on the installment plan, maybe, and settlin' down. Go forth now through all the world and find ye siven beautiful princesses, and the wan of ye that gits the beautifullest shall have the biggest castle."

[NORA *enters, grim.* PAT *notes her demeanor, but concludes comment is unwise. She takes off her bonnet and shawl and goes to her tub, listening to* PAT.]

JIMMIE.

Go on, Paw, what did they do thin?

PAT.

[*Keeping a weather eye on* NORA.]
What did they do thin? Well, they looked and looked fer a year and a day, ivery one o' them in a different counthry, but whiniver one of the siven would be findin' a princess who seemed handsome and likely, whin he looked again careful like, he'd be feared one of his brothers would be findin' a handsomer one, so he'd let her go and move on.

JIMMIE.

An' all the beautiful princesses, weren't there any anywhere no more?

PAT.

[*Slapping his leg in the joy of a sudden inspiration.*]

Faith, Jimmie-boy, it's just comin' into me head what was the throuble! Shure the siven grand princes must 'a' looked in the church window the day I married your Maw, and seein' her that wanst o' course no princess could plaze 'em afther. It was green-eyed envy filled their siven souls that day, I'm thinkin', for Pat O'Flaherty gettin' such a jewell and nobody left beautiful enough for them at all!

JIMMIE.

Paw, quit yer jokin'! Git along with the story.

PAT.

Jimmie darlin', it's not jokin' I am. Your Maw's a jewell, a rael beautiful jewell, and that's the truth. I don't deserve her, I don't. [*Suddenly breaks down and sobs.*]

JIMMIE.

Aw, Paw, don't do that—don't.

[*He begins to whimper.* NORA *starts to comfort him when a knock is heard.* PAT *shakes himself together and opens the door, and* JOHN BING, *a policeman, enters.*]

PAT.

[*To* NORA.]

A policeman!

JOHN BING.

[Glancing at paper in his hand.]
Does Patrick O'Flaherty live here?

PAT.

Faith, he does that, an' what would the majestic arrm o' the law be wantin', if ye please, intrudin' in a peaceful man's house?

JOHN BING.

I've a warrant here for the arrest of Patrick O'Flaherty on the ground of repeated violence towards his wife.

PAT.

Howly Saints! An' who shwore out that warrant?

JOHN BING.

[Glancing at paper.]
Nora O'Flaherty. *[Looking at* NORA.] I guess it's true, all right. Come along.

PAT.

Nora! You niver did that to your own man? [NORA *makes no reply but a sniffle.*] Nora!

JOHN BING.

Well, hurry up. Better come quietly.

JIMMIE.

Paw, what's the matter? What's he come for? Make him go 'way.

PAT.

[*Taking* BING's *coat lapel confidentially.*]
Mr. Officer—you see the little lad there? He's—well—well, he'll never walk no more. Perhaps you got childer yourself? Would you mind just waitin' a bit of a minute, or maybe two, till I finish a shtory I was tellin' him? He'll let me go aisier so.

JOHN BING.

[*Looking at his watch.*]
Five minutes, then.

PAT.

Thank ye kindly. [*Returns to* JIMMIE, *giving his lounge a little push so* JIMMIE *will not see* JOHN BING.] Now, me lad, where were we in the shtory?

JIMMIE.

About the beautiful princesses.

PAT.

Shure, I'm thinkin' it's mortal weary them siven princes will be lookin' for their beautiful princesses all this time, when right here in this room with us two all so happy an' lovin'-like is your Maw, out o' their reach. [JIMMIE *suddenly laughs out merrily, the first time he has done more than smile wanly.*] So what do you think they did next?

JIMMIE

I dunno.

PAT.

Guess.

[*Here* NORA, *who has been weeping and washing harder and harder, makes a dash and throws open the door to the hall, grabbing the warrant meanwhile out of the hand of* JOHN BING.]

NORA.

Mr. Officer, you walk right out o' here and down them shtairs and don't you be waitin' no more for Patrick O'Flaherty. He ain't goin' with you. He's goin' to git a job stiddy and shtay here.

JOHN BING.

You withdraw the charge? I'll have to report it at the station.

NORA.

Charge nothin'! You git out o' here.

JOHN BING.

[*Stopping to gaze at her a moment.*]

Well, what do you think of that? The next time one of them suffragist ladies asks me what I think, I'll tell her I think women is fools, that's what I'll tell her. Yep, all fools! [*He goes out.*]

[PAT *has sat discreetly silent, twirling his thumbs rapidly and looking in front of him.*]

JIMMIE.

Paw! What's Maw talkin' about? What 'u'd he want?

PAT.

Niver you mind, Jimmie-boy. It was just payin' the O'Flaherty family a call he was, nice and friendly like. Your Maw
invited him, but when she saw how dishturbin' his august
prisence was in our happy home, she invited him out again.
Ain't that it, Nora darlin'?

[*He holds out his hand to* NORA. NORA *weakly approaches,
sniffling, then falls on his neck.*]

NORA.

Oh, Pat, Pat! I niver meant to do that awful thing—I niver
did. I dunno what made me. It was that nurse a-talkin' at
me. She put a spell on me, she did. Oh Pat, oh Pat!

PAT.

[*Patting her.*]

Niver mind, niver mind. I know ye didn't. It's all right.
Niver mind, gurrl.

[*A knock at the door.* NORA *pulls herself free and opens
the door to* MISS CARROLL.]

PAT.

[*Retreating.*]

It's that dam' nurse! She'll be the death o' me yit.

Miss Carroll.

[Coming quickly forward towards Jimmie.]

I can't stop a second. I just ran in to tell Jimmie-boy I've been telephoning and it's all fixed. The bran'-new suit's going to happen next Saturday. It's my half-holiday and I'll come for you in a taxi and we'll go down-town and we'll buy it all bran' new to fit, made just for Jimmie.

Jimmie.

Aw! 'tain't so. You're kiddin' me!

Miss Carroll.

'Tis so, honor bright! Cross my heart and hope to die. Well, I must run. *[Suddenly appreciating* Nora's *aspect.]* Why, Mrs. O'Flaherty, what's the matter?

Nora.

The matter is you're a wicked, interferin' woman, a-makin' me do them awful things to me pore man there! Look at him, so sweet and gentle like! Ain't ye 'shamed o' yourself, a-plottin' and workin' to put apart them as God has j'ined together in the howly estate of matrimony? It's a bad, wicked woman I am to be listenin' to your terrible talk. That there horrid big officer in his shiny buttons, lookin' so fat and so satisfied, waitin' there at the door to grab up me pore man hasn't a coat to his back hardly!

Miss Carroll.

What about the boot, Mrs. O'Flaherty?

NORA.

The boot, is it? Shure it's the careless woman I am, happenin' in the way whin he was takin' 'em off and he with a bit of the creature in him made him excited like.

MISS CARROLL.

All right, Mrs. O'Flaherty, I'm sorry. I won't give any more advice. It's against the rules. I shouldn't have said anything. [*She looks at* PAT, *who has been regarding her quizzically while* NORA *holds forth, and now, catching her eye, has the impertinence to wink.* MISS CARROLL *struggles hard not to respond to his grin, but can't quite keep her gravity.*] You see, I haven't any man of my own, so I suppose it's hard for me to understand married life. Good-bye till tomorrow. [*She waves her hand to* JIMMIE, *accomplishes one severe look at* PAT, *and vanishes.* PAT *waves her off gaily.*]

PAT.

Goo'-bye, Miss Carroll, goo'-bye! Goo'-bye! [*He gets his hat and coat, chuckling to himself.*]

JIMMIE.

Did ye hear that, Maw? A bran'-new suit made just for me. Nobody else never wore it at all, an' we'll go in a taxi to buy it on Saturday. Gee! Ain't it nice?

PAT.

[*Sidling up to* NORA *at the tub.*]
Nora darlin', I'm thinkin' it's a foine job I'll be gettin' this day for the askin'; the heart's that big in me for gratitude, it 'll

shine right out through me two eyes and make me hopeful and stiddy-lookin', so that some boss 'll think he's got a grand man to work for him. I'd better be startin' along now, I suppose, er some other chap 'll git there before me. Say, Nora. it's only about twinty cints I do be needin' for carfare.

NORA.

Pat, twinty cents is a lot. Where you goin'?

PAT.

Well, maybe fifteen cints would do if I walk the wan way where there ain't no transfer. Shure it's hard on the poor when the shtreet-car companies git mad at each other. Say, Nora, I know a place where a good job is waitin' for Pat O'Flaherty, but the great city lies between us. Cruel long and wide it is, and hard stones all the way. It's too weary and sad like I'd look on arrivin', an' I couldn't ride on the cars to git there. Oh, come across with the fifteen cents!

[NORA *dubiously gets down an old china teapot from the shelf and takes out five cents, which she gives him gravely. She then gets five cents from another secret place.*]

PAT.

[*As she is getting the money.*]
Faith, there's money all over the place.
[NORA *then gets five pennies from the depths of her pocket and slowly counts out the fifteen cents into his hand.*]

PAT.

[*Kissing her.*]

Oh! That's the shweetest wife ever blessed a bad, bad spalpeen of a husband. Good-bye, gurrl! 'Bye, Jimmie-boy. Be thinkin' what the siven princes could do, they havin' seen your Maw through the church window, and I'll finish the shtory tomorrow.

[PAT *exits,* whistling, NORA *watching him at the door.*]

JIMMIE.

Maw, what's a fool softy?

[NORA *wilts.*]

CURTAIN.

THE
DRAMA CLASS OF TANKAHA, NEVADA

(Written in collaboration with Harriet Calhoun Moss)

Played for the first time on October 23 and 24, 1914, by Mrs. CHAS. ATKINSON, Mrs. CHAS. HUBBARD, Mrs. SAMUEL CHASE, Mrs. HOWARD SHAW, Mrs. LAIRD BELL, Mrs. SAMUEL INSULL, Miss EVELYN SHAW, Mrs. ARTHUR ALDIS, Mr. CHAS. ATKINSON, Mr. DORR BRADLEY, *and* Mrs. HENRY HUBBARD.

THE
DRAMA CLASS OF TANKAHA, NEVADA.

THE PROLOGUE.

CHARACTERS:

MRS. BENNETT, *Hostess of the Class for the Day, a recent arrival in Tankaha, young, well-dressed, progressive.*

MRS. FESSENDEN, *Chairman of the Drama Class, a firm lady, native of Tankaha, with Standards.*

MISS JENNINGS, *Secretary of the Class, unwed and emotional.*

MRS. STEDMAN, *a Mother, pre-eminently.*

MRS. BROKMORTON, *an Aspirant of Culture.*

MISS FESSENDEN, *daughter of* MRS. FESSENDEN, *the Chairman, a young woman struggling under difficulties towards Modernity.*

MRS. BENNETT'S MAID.

Characters of the Play within the Play:

PAOLO......................Mr. Algernon Manning
ANNA, *his wife*...............Miss Sibyl Carrington
MARIO, *his brother*............Mr. Emil Konrad
MADDELENA, *an old family servant*.Miss Frances Nellis

(Taken by members of a theatrical company playing a week's engagement at the Tankaha Opera House.)

SCENE: *The sitting-room of the hostess of the day—*MRS. BENNETT.
*A tastefully furnished apartment, modern; at left (from
audience) a desk or writing-table; at right a sofa; back, a
fireplace; entrance at R. and L.; a few books, photographs,
flowers, etc.*

When the curtain rises MRS. BENNETT, *with the* MAID, *is discovered completing the arrangements to receive the Drama Class.
She puts a small table with paper and pencil in the middle
of the room and counts six seats, three on each side, glances
at the clock.* MRS. *and* MISS FESSENDEN *enter; usual
greetings.*

MRS. BENNETT.

How do you do!   How do you do!   I can't help feeling a little
nervous, entertaining the class for the first time—a new-comer,
you know.

MRS. FESSENDEN.

[*Taking off things.*]

Oh, no need; no need.

MRS. BENNETT.

But you're all so clever, you seem to know just how to look
up everything.   Now I— [*She breaks off to greet new-comers,*
MISS JENNINGS *and* MRS. STEDMAN.]   How do you do!   How
do you do!   Do take off your things, etc., etc. [*Bustle of taking
off wraps, which maid takes away while* MRS. BENNETT *speaks
to* MRS. FESSENDEN.]

MRS. BENNETT.

Madam Chairman, you've no idea the trouble I've had trying
to find out about Giacosa for the class today.   There wasn't

anything about him or by him to be found in Tankaha. At the library they said the only Italian writer that they had was Longfellow's translation of Dante. They told me one of the members of the Board of Trustees had once wanted to buy some of D'Annunzio's plays, but as his resignation was sent in immediately after making the proposal, nothing had been done. [MRS. BROKMORTON *enters*.] Oh, how do you do, Mrs. Brokmorton? [*Glances around*.] I think we are all here, Madam Chairman.

MRS. FESSENDEN.

[*Taking the Chair and picking up gavel*.]

Will the meeting please come to order? We will listen to the minutes of the previous meeting.

[MISS JENNINGS *rises and clears her throat*.]

MISS JENNINGS.

[*Reading*.]

The Drama and Poetry Class of Tankaha Culture Club met on Tuesday, January 10th, at the residence of Mrs. Brokmorton, Mrs. Fessenden, the Chairman, presiding. The minutes of the previous meeting were read and approved, then followed the program for the day, subject, Omar Khayyam, essayist, Mrs. Brokmorton. The paper thoughtfully considered the work of the Persian poet from the standpoint of its influence in the home. Discussion followed:

Mrs. Stedman said that whereas she appreciated the beauty of many of the lines and was glad the Drama Class had chosen it as a subject, she thought it would be unwise to place this poem in the hands of young people.

Miss Fessenden said she thought young people should be allowed to read beautiful literature, no matter what the subject.

Mrs. Bennett thought the philosophy inconclusive, quoting the line "But evermore, came out by the same door wherein I went."

Mrs. Brokmorton, the essayist, said the more she had studied the beautiful quatrains the more she had been convinced that it was extremely difficult for us in America to appreciate and understand the poet's point of view.

Mrs. Fessenden, the Chairman, said it did not surprise her that the poem was sad, when the poet evidently had no religious faith. She then announced the subject of the next meeting —a paper on the Italian dramatist Giacosa, by Mrs. Bennett, the meeting to be held at the home of the essayist of the day on January 24th. On motion the meeting adjourned.

MRS. FESSENDEN.

If there are no objections the minutes will stand approved. They are approved. Are you ready, Mrs. Bennett?

MRS. BENNETT.

[*Rising.*]

Madam Chairman, I started to tell you that I found it very difficult to ascertain anything about Giacosa in Tankaha. Yesterday I learned that one of the members of the company now playing at the Opera House knew of a play by Giacosa. I called on her at the hotel with the result that I have a surprise for you. Four of the members of the company are going to give us this afternoon a short play by Giacosa called "Sacred Ground" right here in this room. [*She stops and looks around*

for encouragement. Stir of excitement and surprise in the class.
MRS. BENNETT *hurries on to explain.*] They said they didn't
need any scenery, and told me how to arrange the room. We
are to go into the dining-room. I thought it was much nicer
than writing a paper on an author I didn't know anything about.
  [MRS. FESSENDEN *and* MRS. STEDMAN *both glance protect-
      ingly at* MISS FESSENDEN.]

MRS. FESSENDEN.

That is very interesting, a surprise indeed. Do you—er—
know anything about the play? It would have been wiser,
perhaps, to consult—

MISS FESSENDEN.

Oh, mamma, it's such a nice plan! [*To* MRS. BENNETT.]
Are they here now? Right here in this house? The actors and
actresses?

MRS. BENNETT.

Yes, they are waiting up-stairs.

MRS. FESSENDEN.

Well, I suppose it is all right, quite a surprise— [*She rises,
as do they all.*]

MRS. BENNETT.

Now please sit there near the doorway.
  [*The ladies step down in front, off stage, some a little dubiously,*
      MISS FESSENDEN *and* MISS JENNINGS *enthusiastically.*]

MRS. BENNETT.

Minnie! [*The* MAID *enters.*] Here, quickly, help me move these things the way I showed you. [*They move chairs off, tables back, etc.*]

[*The* MAID *disappears.* MRS. BENNETT *steps down and joins others.*]

Play follows—"Sacred Ground."

The story is briefly as follows: ANNA *has remained true to* PAOLO, *her husband, in spite of her love for the latter's cousin* LUCIANO, *who has committed suicide just before the play opens, because of her resistance.* PAOLO *discovers the reason for* LUCIANO'S *death through* ANNA'S *letters which he finds on the body and reads. He tries to probe to the depths of his wife's soul. She warns him to desist, finally cries out that she loved* LUCIANO, *and ends by leaving* PAOLO.*

EPILOGUE.

After the Giacosa play ANNA, PAOLO, MARIO *and* MADDELENA *come out to bow to the applause of the Drama Class. The ladies step up on the stage again.* MISS JENNINGS *is sniffling;* MRS. BENNETT *and* MISS FESSENDEN *rush up enthusiastically, the others more slowly.* MRS. FESSENDEN *has paper and pencil in her hand.* MRS. BENNETT *introduces the*

* The play, "Diritti dell Anima," translated by Edith and Allan Updegraff under the title "Sacred Ground," is published by Mitchell Kennerley, New York, in the Modern Drama series. Application to Edwin Bjorkman through the publishers should be made for permission to give a dramatic presentation.

players—"Miss Jennings, Mr. Algernon Manning, Miss Sibyl Carrington, Mrs. Fessenden, our Chairman," etc. Congratulations and general flutter.

MISS CARRINGTON.

You're very kind. Pleasure to play to you! Such a sympathetic audience! So comprehending! It was nothing to "put it over" to you! [*Turns to* MR. MANNING, *snuggling up to him.*] Poor darling! I do treat you atrociously, don't I? But you know I don't mean it! [*Affectionate business between* "ANNA" *and* "PAOLO" *as they disappear.*]

MRS. FESSENDEN.

[*Through her lorgnons.*]
Are they man and wife?

MRS. BENNETT.

I think that—well— Perhaps they're—they're engaged—

MRS. FESSENDEN.

Ladies, the meeting will please come to order for the purpose of discussing the play. [*They move quickly the chairs and tables to their former positions, as in the prologue, and take their places.*] I think we are agreed as to our indebtedness to the essayist of the day, Mrs. Bennett, for arranging the play. We do not need to pass a formal vote of thanks. Our hostess cannot fail to have seen our evident—er—interest. A discussion of the play is now in order. To facilitate this I have jotted down a few questions which occurred to me during the presentation of this—er—unusual play. Here is the first question. [*Reads.*] "Is it to be regretted that Giacosa compressed the material for a rare psychological development into the narrow frame of a single act?"

MRS. BROKMORTON.

[*Rising.*]

Madam Chairman, it seems to me the volcanic character of the problem presented calls for brevity rather than prolixity. The eruption was sudden, torrential, devastating, and does not need, nay, does not permit of elaboration. What would have been gained had we had a preceding act, for instance? Nothing. Had we witnessed the despair and suicide of Luciano the situation would not have been developed more clearly than it was by Paolo's explanation to Mario about the letters. It seems to me this play is a masterpiece of construction; I consider one act is sufficient.

MRS. STEDMAN.

[*Rising very slowly.*]

There is a far more important reason for brevity than construction. Even a one-act play may be one act too long. For a mixed audience, or for innocent young minds, I should suggest the less the better of this sort of food. [*Sits down hard.*]

MRS. FESSENDEN.

I think that this play is strong mental pabulum for any age! We will consider one act is sufficient. [*Picks up paper.*] Here is the second question: "Are Paolo's nature and the quality of his love for Anna above or below those of the average well-bred gentleman of our acquaintance?"

MISS FESSENDEN.

Well, I don't think a well-bred gentleman ought to pry like that.

MISS JENNINGS.

I haven't any husband, of course, but I should think a husband would want to know whether—

MRS. BENNETT.

But she'd done all she could! She'd been faithful, hadn't she? She couldn't help what she felt. What right had he to force her confession?

MRS. FESSENDEN.

Let us put the question in another form first. "Should a wife have a secret of any sort from her husband?"

MRS. STEDMAN.

[*Rising slowly again and commanding attention from her majesty of demeanor.*]
Never! A true wife's mind should be as clear, as transparent as glass, permitting her husband to read every thought. Paolo, the husband, had the right to know!

MRS. BENNETT.

But—but—

MRS. STEDMAN.

Paolo had the right!

MRS. BENNETT.

But the question was—

MISS FESSENDEN.

Yes, yes—whether Paolo— He tormented her—

MRS. BENNETT.

He had no right—

MRS. BROKMORTON.

But let us consider the play as a play.   This is a drama class—
what matter whether he had or he hadn't—

MISS JENNINGS.

It seems to me—

MRS. STEDMAN.

When you are considering a play, such questions as these are
the first to be dealt with!

[*Each interrupted lady mutters the end of her remark, but
not so as to prevent the next one's being heard. An air of
excited confusion prevails, no one listening much to what any
one says.*]

MRS. FESSENDEN.

[*Rapping.*]

Order! We will proceed to the next question.   [*Reads.*] "Do
Latin dramatists give greater importance to—er—what is called
—sex problems [*she brings out the awful word with a distinct effort*]
than those of Teutonic nations?"

MRS. BENNETT.

[Hopping up and instantly beginning. One or two others try to speak, but vainly.]

Isn't it a question of attitude rather than importance? The attitude of the Teutonic dramatists, with the exception of Bernard Shaw and his type, is always one of disapproval, implied or expressed, of all passion, whether licit or illicit. They ignore it, or when they can't ignore it they despise it, whereas the Latin dramatist treats of passion openly and joyously without self-consciousness, as the most exquisite joy—to be grasped whenever and wherever it can be reached. In this instance the author clearly sympathizes with Anna in her regret for her renunciation. Don't you see his play is a protest against the situation in which she finds herself which obliges her to renounce? We may not agree with the author [*somebody exclaims devoutly "I should hope not!"*], but we might at least try to understand his point of view?

[She speaks passionately. As she sits down MISS FESSENDEN, *who is on the edge of her chair, all eagerness, claps her hands softly together in scared approbation. There is a general stir of surprise.]*

MRS. BROKMORTON.

[Rising.]

You mean, of course, merely understanding the point of view, not sympathizing with it?

MISS FESSENDEN.

But if you understand it—how can you help sympathizing? If she loved—

MRS. FESSENDEN.

[*Interrupting.*]

My child! We are getting far from the question [*consults paper*] which related to Latin and Teutonic dramatists. However, let us drop it and proceed to the next, which is important and timely. [*Rapping.*] Here is my next question. [*Reads.*] "Is Anna's attitude towards her husband absolutely right?" "How is it possible that the love of years should have changed to hate in this brief twenty-four hours?"

MISS JENNINGS.

She never loved her husband! She loved Luciano. She not only confessed it, she gloried in it. Don't you remember she said to Paolo, "Couldn't you see I was longing to tell you?" There was no love to change to hate.

MRS. FESSENDEN.

No love? Then why, pray, did she write "I love my husband, I LOVE MY HUSBAND!"

MISS JENNINGS.

But when she wrote that she had not broken the fetters, she was struggling. She loved Luciano, she felt herself yielding, she knew danger was near and so she lied to protect herself, can't you understand?

MRS. BENNETT.

Oh yes, don't you see? It seems to me so clear—

Miss Fessenden.

Oh, mother, I understand her feeling perfectly! She had been repressed so long! She did not dare tell the truth, so she lied hard!

Miss Jennings.

But don't you see—

> [*General confusion—everybody talks at once and excitedly—each one true to type—remarks similar to previous ones. Mrs. Stedman is heard darkly murmuring, "The morals of the youth of Tankaha!"*]

Mrs. Fessenden.

[Raps.]

Order! This question does not admit of discussion. She loved her husband. Here is the last question. *[Reads.]* "When Anna quits the conjugal home for reasons which move us do these reasons also convince us?" Kindly speak one at a time.

Miss Jennings.

They convince me! When love is dead—how could she stay? Don't you remember those beautiful lines:

> "The night has a thousand eyes and the day but one,
>   Yet the light of the whole world dies with the setting sun.
>
> "The mind has a thousand eyes and the heart but one,
>   Yet the light of the whole life dies when love is done."

Miss Fessenden.

Mother, I will speak! I know she never loved her husband— I know she always loved Luciano. I only wish she had gone to

him. It would have been a higher standard of morality. There!
[*She drops into her chair.* MRS. FESSENDEN *opens her mouth, but finds no words.*]

MISS JENNINGS.

Goodness!

MRS. STEDMAN.

[*To* MRS. FESSENDEN.]

That's—what—comes! Maria Fessenden, didn't I tell you two years ago not to let her go to Hindle Wakes?

MRS. BROKMORTON.

But what has all this got to do with the discussion of the play as a play? This is a drama class, not a mothers' meeting.

MRS. BENNETT.

[*A good deal scared, as she knows it is her previous remarks that have inspired* MISS FESSENDEN *to her outburst.*]

To defend and ask comprehension for the attitude of Latin dramatists is a very different thing from—

[*As before each lady continues her views, the separate sentences rising as a bugle-note sounds out above an orchestra.*]

MRS. FESSENDEN.

[*Raps.*]

Ladies, orderly discussion is impossible unless you speak one at a time. My daughter has uttered an extraordinary statement of her views. I should like to ask each member of the class separately whether she agrees with these views. [*Her expression says "dares to agree."*]

Mrs. Brokmorton.

Pardon me, Madam Chairman, but it seems to me your daughter's views as to whether Anna should have gone with Luciano or not are wholly irrelevant. They do not concern us. They are unimportant. Now, Giacosa—

Mrs. Fessenden.

Pardon me, Mrs. Brokmorton, you may be right technically, but I am a mother first, chairman of this class second. There is a far higher question involved than consideration of a play. I shall put the question to each one! [*She fixes* Miss Jennings *with her eye.*] Miss Jennings, do you?

Miss Jennings.

[*With a gulp. She has been weeping off and on from the general intensity and the difficulty of keeping her minutes.*]
No.

Mrs. Fessenden.

Mrs. Stedman, do you?

Mrs. Stedman.

No!!

Mrs. Fessenden.

Mrs. Brokmorton, do you?

Mrs. Brokmorton.

Of course not; but it doesn't matter—

MRS. BENNETT.

[*Badly scared, feeling she has precipitated the row. She wants to say "No," and almost does so, then, recalling she must stand by* MISS FESSENDEN, *she murmurs:*]
I don't think so.

MRS. FESSENDEN.

You don't think so! That means you agree at heart, but don't dare say so? Am I right?

MRS. BENNETT.

No, no! Oh, dear!

MRS. FESSENDEN.

It would seem the younger generation does not know the meaning of the word S-I-N.

[*Hurly-burly begins again.*]

MRS. FESSENDEN.

Order! Order!

CURTAIN.

EXTREME UNCTION

Played for the first time on October 23 and 24, 1914, *by* Miss Isabel McBirney, Miss Volney Foster, Mrs. Edward Pope, Mrs. Henry Hubbard, *and* Mr. Rosecrans Baldwin.

EXTREME UNCTION.

CHARACTERS:

A DYING PROSTITUTE   A SOCIETY LADY
A SALVATION ARMY LASSIE   A DOCTOR
A NURSE

SCENE: *The screened space around a high, narrow bed in a hospital
ward. Record-card hanging above. The screens have anti-
septic white sheets over them.*

*When the curtain rises the nurse is straightening and
tucking in with uncomfortable tightness the white counterpane
of the bed. On the bed, with eyes closed, lies what is left of a
girl of eighteen or twenty. The nurse takes the thermometer
from the girl's mouth, looks at it, shakes her head, and makes
a record note on the chart. She gives the girl water to drink
and leaves her with a final pull to straighten the bedclothes.
The girl tosses restlessly, moans a little and impatiently
kicks at and pulls the bedclothes out at the foot, exclaiming,
"God, I wish they'd lemme 'lone!"*

[THE LADY *enters.*]

THE LADY.

Hattie dear, were you sleeping? No? See, I've brought you
some roses. Aren't they fresh and sweet? Shall I put them in
water?

THE GIRL.

I don' want 'em!

THE LADY.

All right, dear. We'll just put them aside. I know sometimes the perfume is too strong if one isn't quite oneself. Shall I read to you?

THE GIRL.

If you want to.

THE LADY.

What shall I read?

THE GIRL.

I don' care.

THE LADY.

A story, perhaps?

THE GIRL.

All right—fire it off.

THE LADY.

And then afterwards, Hattie dear, perhaps if you'd let me, the twenty-third psalm. It's so gentle and quiet! You might go to sleep—and when you awakened you'd hear those comforting words.

THE GIRL.

Is that the one about the valley? God, but I'm sick of it!
Gives me the jimmies. Got a story?

[THE LADY *puts the flowers back in their box—takes off her
wrap and settles herself to read aloud from a magazine.*

Marianna Lane swung back and forth, back and forth, in the hammock, tapping her small, brown toe on the porch as she swung. It
was a charming porch, framed in clematis and woodbine, but
Marianna had no eye for its good points. She was lying with two
slim arms clasped behind her head, staring vacantly up at the
ceiling and composing a poem. On the wicker table beside her stood
a glass of malted milk and a teaspoon. They were not the subject
of the poem, but they were nevertheless responsible for it. Her
cousin Frank, who lived in the next house, had been inspired to
make up an insulting ditty.

"Grocerman, bring a can
Baby-food for Mary Ann!"

[THE GIRL *listens for a moment with a faint show of interest,
then goes back to her restless tossing.*]

THE GIRL.

[*Interrupting.*]
Say, d'ye know I'm done for?

THE LADY.

Oh no! You're getting better every day.

THE GIRL.

Oh, quit it! I'm goin', I tell ye. I've got a head-piece on me,
haven't I? I can tell—they've stopped doin' all them things to

me. The doctor just sets down there where you are and looks at me—and, say—he's got gump, that doctor. He's the only one knows I know.

THE LADY.

You mustn't talk like that. I'm sure you're going to get well. [*Girl makes an angry snort.*] Now try and lie quiet. You mustn't get excited, you know, it isn't good for sick people. I'll go on with the story. You'll see. Now listen, will you, dear? It's quite interesting. [*Reads.*]

> " Grocerman, bring a can
> Baby-food for Mary Ann!"

he sang loudly over the hedge whenever he caught sight of Marianna's middy blouse and yellow pigtails. That was yesterday. To-day the malted milk was standing untouched upon the wicker table, and Marianna in the hammock was trying to think up an offensive rhyme for Frank. When she found it, she intended to go around on the other side of the house and shout it as loud as ever she could in the direction of her uncle's garden. This, it is true, was a tame revenge. What Marianna really wanted to do was to go over and pinch her cousin Frank; but that, unhappily, was out of the question, as Frank had a cold, and she was strictly forbidden to go near anybody with a cold.*

THE GIRL.

[*Interrupting.*]

Lady, where d' you think you're goin' to when you kick it? Tell me!

THE LADY.

Why—I don't know— To Heaven, I hope—but you mustn't—

* From *The Century*, March, 1914.

THE GIRL.

What makes you think you're goin' to Heaven?

THE LADY.

Well—I think so because—well—because I've always tried to do right—no, no—I didn't mean that exactly. Of course I've done millions of wrong things—but I mean— Oh, Hattie dear, Heaven is such a vague term! All we know is that it is a beautiful place where we'll be happy, and that we're going there.

THE GIRL.

How do you know we're goin'?

THE LADY.

I don't know. I believe.

THE GIRL.

But how do you know the wrong things you done won't keep you out?

THE LADY.

Now I'm afraid you're exciting yourself—

THE GIRL.

Oh, Lord, cut that out! I'm excited, all right, all right! Guess you'd be if you had the thoughts I got goin' 'round in your head all the time—but there's no sense talkin' them out. Nobody can't do nothin' for me now!

THE LADY.

Oh, you mustn't say that!

THE GIRL.

Well, can ye?

THE LADY.

I'll try, if you will tell me what is troubling you.

THE GIRL.

Oh, Gawd!   She wants to know what's troublin' me, she does!

THE LADY.

Can't you tell me?   Perhaps I could help you.

THE GIRL.

You said you done wrong things.   What was they?

THE LADY.

I—I don't know exactly.

THE GIRL.

You don't know?

THE LADY.

Why, I suppose I could think of lots of things, but—

THE GIRL.

She could "think of lots o' things"!   Has to stop to remember.
Oh, gee!   Guess she'll get in.

The Lady.

Oh, please don't laugh like that! Listen! Whatever you have done, no matter how dreadful, if you are sorry it will be all right. Don't be afraid.

The Girl.

Is that true?

The Lady.

Yes.

The Girl.

I don't believe it.

The Lady.

It is true, nevertheless.

The Girl.

Well, if you ain't sorry?

The Lady.

But surely you are—you must be!

The Girl.

No, I ain't. It was better dead.

The Lady.

What do you mean?

The Girl.

I tell ye, it was better to be dead. Say, Lady—in them wrong things you done you can't remember did ye—did ye ever kill a kid that hadn't hardly breathed? Say, did ye—did ye?

THE LADY.

Oh, oh! What shall I do? Hattie! Hattie! Try and stop crying. I'm so grieved for you. Tell me what you wish—only don't cry so!

THE GIRL.

I ain't sorry.

THE LADY.

No, no, never mind that. Tell me if you want to, tell me—about it.

THE GIRL.

An' I ain't sorry for what cum first—him—it was all I ever had that time, that little, weeny time!

THE LADY.

Wait a moment—wouldn't you rather have a clergyman?

THE GIRL.

No! There's one comes 'round here. I don' want to tell him nothin'.

THE LADY.

Very well—go on.

THE GIRL.

It was so little, and it squawked! It squawked awful!

THE LADY.

Oh don't!

THE GIRL.

You don't want me to tell ye?

THE LADY.

Yes, yes.

THE GIRL.

Oh, what's the use? What's the use? You can't do nothin'. Nobody kin. I ain't sorry! The kid's better dead, lots better. It's what cum after. I'm so dirty! I'm so dirty! I'll never get clean! Oh, what's gona happen when I die? What's gona happen? An' I gotta die soon!

THE LADY.

You mustn't feel so; you mustn't! God is kind and good and merciful. He will forgive you. Ask Him to!

THE GIRL.

I did ask Him to—lots o' times. It don' do no good. I ain't sorry! Everybody says you gotta feel sorry, an' I ain't. A girl kid's better dead, I tell ye! That's why I done it. I loved it, 'fore it came, 'cause it was his'n. After I done it nothin' mattered—nothin'! So I— And I gotta die soon. What's gona happen?

[*During the preceding the sound of a tambourine and singing has been heard outside. As* THE GIRL *cries out the last words* THE LADY, *finding no answer, goes to the window. She has a sudden thought.*]

THE LADY.

I'll be back in a moment! [*She goes out.*]

  [*Nothing is heard but* THE GIRL'S *sobs for a moment.   Then*
    THE LADY *ushers in a* SALVATION ARMY LASSIE, *her
    tambourine held tightly, but jingling a little.   She stands
    embarrassed by the foot of the bed.*   THE GIRL *stares at her.*]

THE GIRL.

I know them kind, too.

THE LASSIE.

Can't I do something for you?

THE GIRL.

No—not now. You're a good sort enough—but—I ain't
sorry— I tell ye—I ain't, I ain't!

THE LASSIE.

[*To* LADY.]
What d' ye want me for? What 'll I do?

THE LADY.

Couldn't you sing something brave and cheerful? You were
singing so nicely out there.

THE LASSIE
[*To* GIRL.]

Shall I?

THE GIRL.

No, they won't let ye. It 'u'd make a noise.

THE LADY.

Sing it low.

THE LASSIE.

[*In a sing-song voice, swaying, half chanting, half speaking.*]
Shall we gather at the river—the beautiful, the beautiful river, etc.

THE GIRL.

[*After trying to listen for a stanza or two.*]
Oh, cut it out! I don't want ye to sing to me. I want ye to tell me what's gona happen. Oh, don' nobody know? I'm so 'fraid—so 'fraid!

[*As her voice rises the nurse, who has, unobserved, looked in during the singing, enters with* THE DOCTOR. *He bows slightly to* THE LADY *and* THE LASSIE, *then goes quickly to* THE GIRL, *putting his hand on her forehead.*]

THE DOCTOR.

Why, child, what troubles you?

THE GIRL.

[*Clinging to his hand.*]
Doctor! Everybody says I got to be sorry to get in. I ain't sorry, an' I'm 'fraid, I'm 'fraid.

THE DOCTOR.

To get in where?

THE GIRL.

Heaven, where you'll be happy.

THE DOCTOR.

That is very interesting. How do you suppose they found that out? How do they know, I mean?

THE LADY.

Doctor, I didn't tell her that.

THE DOCTOR.

Didn't you? She seems strangely excited. [*He seats himself by the bed.*] Come, child, let's talk about it.

[*He motions to the nurse that she is not needed. She goes out. THE SALVATION ARMY LASSIE makes an awkward little bow and gets herself out. THE LADY stands at the foot of the bed listening for a few moments, then slips quietly out.*]

THE DOCTOR.

Now, tell me what is on your mind. But try and stop crying and speak plainly, for I want to understand what you say.

THE GIRL.

I'm gona die, ain't I?

THE DOCTOR.

Yes.

THE GIRL.

When?

THE DOCTOR.

I don't know.

THE GIRL.

Soon?

THE DOCTOR.

Yes.

THE GIRL.

How soon?   Tomorrow?

THE DOCTOR.

No, not tomorrow.   Perhaps in a month, perhaps longer.

THE GIRL.

Will I get sorry 'fore I go?

THE DOCTOR.

How can I tell?   But what does it matter?   Why do you want to be sorry especially?   What good would it do?   It is all passed, isn't it?   Nothing can change that.

THE GIRL.

But I gotta be—to get in.

THE DOCTOR.

You seem very sure on that point.

THE GIRL.

But everybody says I gotta be.

THE DOCTOR.

What is the use saying it or thinking it when nobody knows?

THE GIRL.

What you sayin'?

THE DOCTOR.

You and I can believe differently if we want to. But why in the world should you be asking me all these hard questions? I've never been to heaven, have I? I don't know whether you have to be sorry to get in or not. How do you suppose they found all that out?

THE GIRL.

But ain't I gotta be punished somewhere till I git sorry?

THE DOCTOR.

Do you remember the other night when the pain was so bad?

THE GIRL.

Yep.

THE DOCTOR.

And I told you you would have to bear it, that I could do nothing for you, and that you must be quiet, not to disturb the others?

THE GIRL.

Oh, don't I remember!

THE DOCTOR.

I guess that's about enough punishment for one little girl. You've been pretty unhappy lately, haven't you, with the pain and the terrible thoughts? I think it's about time something else turned up for you that would be nicer, don't you?

THE GIRL.

Turned up?

THE DOCTOR.

Yes, something that would make up for all this. Do you know, child, as I've gone through these wards day after day 'tending to all you sick folks I've about come to the conclusion that there must be—something nicer—

THE GIRL.

Tell me more about it.

THE DOCTOR.

Well, now—there's another queer question. Didn't I tell you I don't know anything to tell? I've never been there. I should think you would have found out a little something, since you're planning to go so soon. But no, I don't suppose you know much more than the rest of us. And when you get there you will probably forget all about me and how much I'd like to know what's happening to my little patient. No use, I suppose, asking you to tie a red string on your finger and say, "That's to send Dr. Carroll a little message." Is there any way, do you think you could remember?

THE GIRL.

You're kiddin' me!

THE DOCTOR.

Indeed I am not. I long to know with all my heart, and I suppose it will be years and years before I do. Why, just think, you—you, are going to have a great adventure. You are going on a journey to a far country where you'll find out lots of things, and here am I, jogging along up and down, to and fro, between my office and this hospital, and wondering and wondering and wondering! What a lucky little girl you are!

THE GIRL.

And I don't have to be sorry—to git in?

THE DOCTOR.

Didn't I tell you you were going soon, anyway? You can be sorry if you want to—but I think it is more interesting to dream about the strange things there will be to discover at the end of the journey.

THE GIRL.

Will there be gates of gold that open wide, and angels standin' by with shinin' wings?

THE DOCTOR.

Wouldn't you like to know? And so would I. You mustn't forget to send that message. Will you? Do be careful to be accurate and try to speak distinctly. You know that a great many wise men have promised to send messages back, yet all that seems to come are foolish words. If you will look at everything carefully and find a way of telling me, I'll write it down for all the world to ponder. Oh—then we should really know something—not just be groping—groping—groping in the dark. If you only could, if you only could! I wonder— [*In his turn he gazes at her intently, then rises abruptly.*] Well, child, I must go on. Shall I teach you a few questions before you go, so you'll be sure and find out for me the most important things?

THE GIRL.

Oh, Doctor!

THE DOCTOR.

You'd like to do something for me, wouldn't you, child? [THE GIRL *reaches out for his hand and kisses it humbly, then gazes at him.*]

THE DOCTOR.

Well, that would be the most wonderful thing in the world, only you must be very, very careful, and you must do a lot of thinking before you go, about what I've said. It is important to understand. Don't waste any time thinking about what is passed, will you?

THE GIRL.

No, Doctor.

THE DOCTOR.

We must talk it all over. There aren't many people I could trust to remember exactly all the things I want to know. But you can if you try hard. [*He touches the bell; the nurse appears.*] Now, Miss Bryant, Miss Hattie and I have several important things to discuss and there isn't much time left, so if she wants me at any time call me and I'll come. And I think while she has so much thinking on hand about what I'm asking her to do for me, she had better not see other visitors. You don't mind, do you?

The Girl.

No, no! I don' want 'em! Doctor, when will it come? Doctor, will I know soon?

The Doctor.

Soon, I think; very soon. [*He takes her hand a second, then goes out, motioning the nurse to precede him.*]

The Girl.

Soon! He said it would be very soon—and I'm so tired! I'd like something nicer. [*She settles herself with a little sigh, and falls asleep.*]

CURTAIN.

THE LETTER

Played for the first time on August 18 and 19, 1915, by Mr. CHAS. ATKINSON, Mr. ERNST VON AMMON, *and* Mr. JOHN ROOT.

THE LETTER.

CHARACTERS:

> HORACE TANNER.
> JOHN ROBERTS.
> BELL-BOY.

TIME: *Midnight of a summer night. Present day.*

SCENE: *Writing-room of a club. Entrances at back and right.*
When the curtain rises the two men are seated on opposite sides of the room, facing away from each other. HORACE TANNER is occupied in opening, throwing away or laying aside a pile of mail which is on the writing-table before him. JOHN ROBERTS is writing a letter, which he folds, seals and addresses. Finding himself without a stamp, he leaves the room, back. Neither man is conscious of the other's presence. TANNER starts to answer a note, refers to a letter he has put aside, then lets his pen drop and stares in front of him listlessly. He is a man between thirty-five and forty with a clean-cut fine face. The jaw is square, the eyes and brow those of a dreamer.

[The BELL-BOY *enters.]*

BELL-BOY.

This Mr. Tanner, sir?

TANNER.

Yes. What is it?

BELL-BOY.

Letter for you, sir. [*Holds out a tray with a long sealed envelope.*]

TANNER.

I got my mail at the desk when I arrived. Where was this?

BELL-BOY.

It is a registered letter, sir. The clerk always keeps 'em in the safe.

TANNER.

I see. Thank you.

[*The* BELL-BOY *goes out.* TANNER *opens the envelope slowly, after looking curiously at the handwriting. Inside is another envelope of which the seal has been broken. Around this is a half-sheet of note-paper. At the handwriting on the second envelope* TANNER *gives a start. He glances at the note, then throws it aside and becomes absorbed in the contents of the inner envelope. The letter he reads is not long, perhaps four or five pages. He turns it over and over, trying to find more. He has laid the envelope, the one on which the writing has startled him, beside him on the desk. As he reads, leaning forward, the envelope is pushed by his elbow onto the floor and lies there unnoticed.* TANNER *is so absorbed he does not notice or look up as* ROBERTS *re-enters from back.* ROBERTS *is a man of address and strength. His mouth has set lines around it. He is, perhaps, forty-five to fifty. He is dressed in mourning and looks careworn. As he enters, a lighted cigar is in his hand, but it is soon put down and forgotten. He thinks he recog-*

nizes TANNER, *then sees he is mistaken. He is about to return to his desk when his eye falls on the envelope on the floor. He picks it up courteously, saying, "I beg your pardon."* TANNER *does not hear him. As* ROBERTS *places the envelope on the table he sees the handwriting. He is plainly amazed and glances sharply at* TANNER, *who is still re-reading the letter.*]

ROBERTS.

That is my wife's handwriting. She is dead. The name on the envelope, James Douglas, is that of a friend of hers and of mine. You have a letter there in the same handwriting. Where did you get it?

[TANNER *holds the letter tightly in his left hand and makes no answer.*]

ROBERTS.

Where did you get it?

TANNER.

I decline to answer.

ROBERTS.

The letter does not belong to you.

[*For answer* TANNER *folds it, puts it in his pocket, rises and bows.*]

TANNER.

I will bid you good-night.

ROBERTS.

Not until you have explained how you come to have my wife's letter in your possession, and why you were so absorbed in it as not to hear me when I spoke.

TANNER.

Why should I answer when you have no right to ask me the question?

ROBERTS.

No right! Was she not my wife?

TANNER.

No.

ROBERTS.

How do you know that?

TANNER.

Again I decline to answer.

ROBERTS.

Did you know my wife?

TANNER.

You mean Mrs. Roberts? Yes.

ROBERTS.

You know the person to whom the letter is directed?

TANNER.

No.

ROBERTS.

Yet you will not explain?

TANNER.

I see no obligation to do so

ROBERTS.

Was the letter sent you?

TANNER.

Presumably, or given.   One does not steal letters.

ROBERTS.

Can you not understand how it is that I should feel I had the right to ask an explanation?

TANNER.

Well, to be frank, I cannot.   In my code, which no doubt is peculiar, no one has rights over another, even when that other is living—when he is dead still less.   That the woman who bore your name wrote a letter to a friend, of which you were ignorant, is a sufficient reason for me to desire to protect its contents now from your curiosity.   [TANNER *gathers up his papers.*]

ROBERTS.

Admitting that I have not the right, have you?   If you have, how came you by it?

TANNER.

You forget that I answer only such of your questions as I choose to answer. I think we had better say good-night. [*He moves towards the door, right.*]

ROBERTS.

Wait! You have convinced me that the question of rights is not one to raise now. May there not be other questions involved, of kindness, of consideration, of humanity? If I ask you, to give me easement of pain, ask it as one human being in distress cries out to another, what will you say then?

TANNER.

Merely that in this particular instance the justice of withholding is more important than the doubtful "kindness," as you call it, of giving.

    [ROBERTS *turns away and bows his head, then sits down at the writing-table and tries to write. His distress is so genuine that for the first time* TANNER *shows an interest in him.*]

TANNER.

This talk is becoming painful to us both. It had better be ended. You ask information which I cannot give. Let the matter end there.

ROBERTS.

Will you tell me your name?

TANNER.

I have no reason for not doing so.   Horace Tanner.

ROBERTS.

[Glancing at him as if the name were familiar.]

You are Horace Tanner, and you have in your possession a letter from my wife addressed to James Douglas? Mr. Tanner, you and I have met under extraordinary circumstances, and spoken together as men speak once or twice in a lifetime. It is not possible for us to part now—that is, it is not possible for me, with no further speech. I acknowledge that I exceeded my rights in demanding an explanation. I want to win your acquiescence by another method. Evidently you know something of what lay between my wife and myself. Until tonight I thought no one knew. *[A pause.]* I will tell you the story if you wish.   Shall I?

[TANNER walks backwards and forwards behind ROBERTS, who is seated. It is evidently a difficult decision. ROBERTS is not looking at him. ROBERTS' eyes are downcast, as he is embarrassed with his own offer.]

ROBERTS.

[Over his shoulder.]

If you say no, there is nothing left but to bid each other good-night.   In that case, I shall have an additional weight to carry, when it often seems to me the one I have is too heavy to be borne.

TANNER.

Go on—speak.
[*There is a pause while each man seems to gather himself together.* TANNER *seats himself, right desk.*]

ROBERTS.

It is very extraordinary for me to find myself bidden to speak at my own solicitation, of matters which a half-hour since I should have said would be forever hidden, yet when one has upon one's mind, day and night, waking and sleeping, one all-pervading thought, silence becomes an unbearable torment. Under such circumstances, even the dumb must speak.

TANNER.

I understand—go on.

ROBERTS.

In spite of our grim words just now, demanding and denying, something in you makes me willing to speak. May I ask you one question?

TANNER.

Yes, with the provision I need not answer it.

ROBERTS.

You would not allow me to use the words "my wife." Did your knowledge come from her?

TANNER.

During the time I knew her, you mean?
[ROBERTS *bows his head in assent.*]

TANNER.

No, it did not.

ROBERTS.

[*Springing from his chair, threateningly.*]
What was there between you?   Tell me!

TANNER.

To use your own term, you have no right to ask me that.

ROBERTS.

O God, don't hurl that at me over and over again.   [*He goes to back of stage.*]

TANNER.

You were going to tell me a story?

ROBERTS.

Yes, I was, and I will.   Forgive me—I'll not lose my self-control again.   [*There is a short pause during which* ROBERTS *makes an effort for calmness, and* TANNER *watches him quietly.*] We were married eighteen years ago. She was nineteen, I thirty.   We had known each other only a few months.   She cared for me then—I know she did—I know it.   For a few years there was happiness.   There were the boys.   She seemed absorbed in them. They were sturdy chaps. Then they went to school. That was five years ago. It was ghastly—not having them. For a long time we had not been much together. I never asked myself if she was happy. She seemed so. I suppose I wasn't particularly, but I hadn't time to think about it. I was away a good deal. We never seemed to have much to say to each other. She told me once that never in our whole married life had I asked her what she was thinking about. It only came back to me, afterwards—what she meant, I mean. I suppose she was lonely. [TANNER *bows his head in acquiescence.* ROBERTS *looks at him and sees he understands.*] Well, after the boys went away there came a kind of crisis. Nothing definite. We never said anything to each other about our own situation. Gradually we had become entirely separated. I thought I had better get away. A friend was going to Italy, so I proposed to join him. She urged my going, saying I needed a holiday and that she was perfectly well. I was anxious at first, but her letters came regularly and sounded cheerful. I stayed abroad almost a year, first in Italy and Greece, then to India, then back to Italy. I was in London, wondering whether to come home or go back to the continent, when I heard, not from her, but from an acquaintance I ran into, that she was ill. A great longing came over me to see her—to take care of her. Why had she not told me? What was the matter? I cabled, and sailed at once. A month after I got home she died.

TANNER.

[*After waiting a moment.*]

I think I can understand. It's a pretty tragic story, and, I imagine, not an uncommon one. I fancy among people of our class, silence causes more trouble than speech. May I ask you a question? Did you have any intimate conversation with her before she died—about the past, I mean?

ROBERTS.

Yes, a little. I think she knew how I loved her. When I got home she said she had been ill, but was better. Shortly after she had a trifling operation from which she didn't rally. She seemed to want to have me with her—but—I couldn't hold her—it was too late—too late!

TANNER.

A strange nature!

ROBERTS.

When I began to speak it was with the intention and hope of making you do the same. As I think over the past, the difficulties she must have met are clear to me. I have been very dull and blind. Speaking about these things has been a relief. Everything seems plainer to me now. Mr. Tanner, I want to say this to you, if you knew her, if your friendship made her happier, why, I am glad.

TANNER.

I did know her, the winter you were abroad. We were a great deal together. It was a rare friendship, a peculiarly vivid and stimulating one for me. She had a rich nature full of surprises, and perhaps I may have drawn from her more than had been demanded before. I am a taxing friend, Mr. Roberts.

[ROBERTS *rises*.]

ROBERTS.

I have given you my confidence, Mr. Tanner.

TANNER.

And I will be equally frank. If you still wish it, I will read the letter to you, but I will warn you first that you will find it extraordinarily painful.

ROBERTS.

That doesn't matter now. Read it, please.

TANNER.

[*Taking out the letter from his pocket.*]
I have never received anything in my life that has touched me more profoundly. I am awed by it. I feel as if I should touch the very paper with reverence.

ROBERTS.

May I have it? [ROBERTS *stands with his back to* TANNER *and with his arms folded.*]

TANNER.

[*Unfolds the letter slowly.*]
The letter reached me only tonight by registered mail. I have been away. There was a note from James Douglas. [*Reads.*]

DEAR MR. TANNER:

I am discharging a sacred obligation in sending you the enclosed. I need not tell you that the confidence given me is equally sacred.

Yours truly,

JAMES DOUGLAS.

ROBERTS.

I understand—go on.

TANNER.

[Reading.]

Oh Jim, dear old Jim—I am so wildly happy tonight I must talk to someone, and you're such a good friend! If you were only here! Such a wonderful thing has happened to me, Jim—such a strange, exalting, beautiful thing. I did not know love was like this—I did not know anyone could be so happy— [TANNER *glances at* ROBERTS, *uncertain whether he can go on, then continues*] for I'm in love, Jim dear, in love, like a girl of eighteen. There, I've said it and I dare say it again—I'm in love. I love him! I love him! I love him! and if I must suffer all the rest of my life, still I shall have known what love meant, for I never have, Jim—never.

I turn to you, my old friend, because I have no one else, no one to whom I can speak, and that which is in my heart will not be held in. Oh, I know it's mad, wild folly. It will mean dreadful pain somewhere ahead—but tonight, tonight is mine! and I can fling out my arms to the stars and sing and shout with the joy and the glory and the beauty. We have been together all day, talking, talking, talking, there was so much to say, and now I can hear his grave voice, his sudden laugh—I can feel the pressure of his hand as he said good-night. He is coming again tomorrow and we are going to take our lunch and go for a long tramp, and for a day the world, the whole wide world will be ours.

Oh Jim, I think I've been waiting for him all my life. I didn't even know I was waiting—I didn't know I lived in fog and mist and darkness until this great golden light burst in.

Of course there's pain to come—but I'll bear it, Jim. I can, because I've had these two days, and I won't cry out. I can be very still. I know there can be nothing ahead, nothing, but I shall always be stronger, bigger, wiser and more tender because I have known this. Oh Jim, I have been so lonely! The long days, the long nights alone, always alone. They have been hard to bear. I shall go on with my life, and, Jim—no one but you shall know what has come to be.

Shall I send this letter? I don't even know where you are—I don't think I've been really writing to you. I've been writing to him. I wrote "Jim," and I meant "Horace." I see that now—but he must never know, he must not. It would make things too difficult, and that is all that you shall know about him—just his name, but if I should die there would be no harm in his knowing then, would there? I think he would be glad. I'll put the address in this little envelope and seal it and if I should die send him this letter. It is more his than yours.

[ROBERTS *has listened without a sound, scarcely a change of expression—motionless. There is a pause.*]

ROBERTS.

I am glad—she had—those—two days. They weren't much, were they? And I never knew, I never knew—anything! Yet I loved her. She was the only woman that ever came into my life. She knew that—at the end—knew how deeply I loved her, I mean. She seemed glad to know it. She asked me once if I had been happy, if she had made me happy—asked it with her eyes fixed on mine. When I said yes she dropped back on the pillow. I remember it so well, and I didn't know, I didn't know! [*He sits down.*] Oh how blind, how blind!

You must have loved her dearly. If I had only known!
[TANNER *is silent.*] You did love her? [TANNER *makes no reply.*] Man! you did love her?

TANNER.

We were great friends—

ROBERTS.

Yes, yes, of course, but—after that letter was written—what happened?

TANNER.

We saw each other often. I told you she was a wonderful friend.

ROBERTS.

But—but you loved her, [*rises*] didn't you? She had a little happiness? Tell me! Tell me! I must know.

TANNER.

What is love? We had some golden days together, then I had to go away—I heard of her death when I was on the other side of the world. As I told you, this letter reached me only tonight. I found it here.

ROBERTS.

You never knew that she loved you?

TANNER.

Sometimes I guessed—but it seemed so incredible—I couldn't believe— We never spoke—

ROBERTS.

Give me the letter.

TANNER.

No.

ROBERTS.

You shall. It is not yours— You did not love her.

TANNER.

It is mine. It's a wonderful letter— It is precious to me.

ROBERTS.

Why?

TANNER.

You forget that I am a novelist.

[*The two men stand facing each other.*]

ROBERTS.

Why! What do you mean?

TANNER.

I wondered whether you would strike me, but you do not even understand. I suppose it would be impossible to explain. Do not think that I mean to use these precious words as—copy. That man, her old friend, said they were "sacred"— Well, they are to me, too. I could find it in my heart to envy the feeling they portray. Just now, when you were telling your story, I wondered whether the man who could not express what he felt, or the man who expressed it too well, had loved her best.

ROBERTS.

Still I do not understand.

TANNER

No, nor ever will! But at least in your sorrow you can be simple, you are not tormented with the desire, with the necessity of writing it down, of giving it forth for the world to misunderstand and gape at. Oh, what am I that a woman should love me? I, the mountebank, the actor, the reproducer, who feeds on life only to turn it into art? [*He stands with the letter in his hands, looking at it; then suddenly holds it out to Roberts.*] I will give you the letter, Mr. Roberts. I have read it twice, its sweet phrases are mine now, mine for always. Today I think that I shall never use them, but I shall. In spite of myself, sometime the story of those golden days will be written, will write itself, and you will cringe as you read the pages, for you do not know that every novel, every poem, every play that is written holds a tragedy of sacrifice. Some one must bleed, some one must be hurt, some one must die; it all goes into the crucible, and when the book is closed and put back upon the shelf, when the curtain comes down upon the play, who knows what has gone before, who knows, who knows?

ROBERTS.

You loved her?

TANNER.

Yes,— In my fashion.

ROBERTS.

I think I understand something of what you mean, but what does it matter? She is no longer yours nor mine.

[*Roberts turns to the desk and picks up his papers as the curtain falls.*]

TEMPERAMENT

A Musical Tragedy in Two Scenes

Played for the first time on October 25, 1915, by Mr. BEN-JAMIN CARPENTER, Mrs. CHARLES ATKINSON, *and* Mrs. ARTHUR ALDIS.

TEMPERAMENT.

A Musical Tragedy in Two Scenes.

Characters:

> Hugh Irwin, *a Musician.*
> Annabelle Irwin, *his wife.*
> Gladys Huntington, *an Actress.*

Time: *The present.*

Scene I: *Library of the Irwins' house in the country, simply and tastefully furnished. Black and white and rose idea—one blue jar, etc. A piano closed and covered with an embroidery—flowers about. An air of comfort and dainty luxury. The time is ten o'clock of a winter's evening. A wood fire crackles behind bright brasses.*

When the curtain rises Annabelle *is seated by the fire under a rose-shaded lamp, sewing. Now she is plump and charming. Later on she will be too stout. She holds up a child's frock of light-blue material and examines it critically, then pounces on an unfinished spot and sets to work.* Hugh Irwin *on the other side of the room has been reading "The Nation." He puts it down once or twice and regards* Annabelle *over his eye-glasses as if desiring to speak, in fact he gets as far as opening his mouth, but, seeing her preoccupation, gives it up and attacks "The Nation" with renewed determination. Finally he slaps it down.*

HUGH.

Why in thunder don't you say something?

ANNABELLE.

[With five pins between her lips.]
Haven't anything to say. Why don't you?

HUGH.

Can't you make up something?

ANNABELLE.

[Pinning intently.]
In a minute! In a minute! This is so puzzling! Now I
thought I had the front part of that yoke— *[Her voice trails
off in a soliloquy about the intricacies of little girls' frocks. Finally
with a "ha" of satisfaction she lays it in her lap and comes to.]*
What was that you said, dear? Make up something! What
a funny idea! You're just like baby Gertrude! What do you
want me to say? I can't think of anything. *[She looks long-
ingly at the frock and sneaks in another pin.]*

HUGH.

You might tell me my faults.

ANNABELLE.

Your faults? Why, my dear! *[Pins more happily and
frankly.]* You haven't any! At least if you have I don't see
them. *[Her voice indicates she is talking with the top of her mind.]*

Hugh.

Good Lord! [*He takes up "The Nation" again, then drops it.*] You mean I have so many you can't be bothered trying to enumerate them?

Annabelle.

No, no, not at all. Let me see. Sometimes, oh very rarely, but just sometimes, I've thought if you could be a little tidier—not drop everything about, anywhere;. and then sometimes, since you're asking me, if I could know within an hour or so when you are coming to meals it would be a little more convenient, in the housekeeping, you know. I mean, of course, nicer for you; I don't mind. That's all I can think of—and of course I wouldn't have said anything unless you'd asked. Oh, Hugh, I'm afraid I've been unkind. Have I? Oh do say I haven't! It doesn't matter much about the meals, truly it doesn't; just on your account, that's all.

Hugh.

Always on my account! Always fussing about me! Good Lord! haven't you got any opinions of your own? Don't you ever think of anything more interesting than what to get for my dinner? Great Scott!

Annabelle.

But, Hugh, it makes me so happy to think about what you'd like for your dinner! I know I have lots of faults, yes, of course I must have, but I do try to be a good housekeeper, and I think I am. What other faults have I got?

HUGH.

Hm! Faults! I guess perhaps it's your virtues, then! There are too many of them. They stick out all over you like pins on the pink pin-cushion in the guest-room. In the first place, I'd like to know why you don't grow old. You're too darn good-looking. You're just as soft and pink and white and dimpled as when I married you ten years ago. It's outrageous!

[ANNABELLE *picks up the frock and purrs softly up at him with an adoring smile.*]

ANNABELLE.

Go on.

HUGH.

In the second place, you make me too damn comfortable. My clothes are always brushed and laid out just right. If I don't want to dress, they vanish. Dinner is always ready any time, hot and delicious and too much of it! Other people's cooks leave, but ours are marvels and stick. There's never a sound in the house when I'm composing or practising. I never know when the piano-tuner comes, but the piano is always perfect. You never ask for more allowance, and the children never howl. But what—what about me? It's awful! I'm getting fat! And my music! It's getting fat, too. It waddles and clucks and cackles like a stuffed goose. And my soul, it's growing fat—too fat to soar. Oh, it's killing me—it's killing me!

ANNABELLE.

[*Taking all the pins out of her mouth.*]

Hugh! are you serious? I think your music is perfectly beautiful. You know I do.

HUGH.

Perfectly serious. I'm stifled, I tell you. I'm gasping for
air. You smother me with comfort and ease and adoration.
I'm dying of it, and, what's worse, the heart, the core, the essence
of me, the music I might have written! It's dead too! Oh,
it's awful, awful! [*He paces the room like a caged tiger.*]

ANNABELLE.

[*Watching him for a while.*]
I see, I see it all, and I've been trying so hard for ten years
to make you comfortable! Why didn't you tell me before you
didn't want to be comfortable? And what do you want me to
do now? I'll try to be different. I won't take so much pains
keeping the meals hot and the children quiet. I'll do all I can.

HUGH.

Oh no, no, that isn't what I mean. You're adorable, of
course, perfectly adorable, but—if you could, Annabelle—I suppose it's absurd to ask—but if you could be a little more romantic,
Annabelle—just a little, you know! Do you think you could?
Just now when I asked you to go out into the great still whiteness
out there, to feel the sting and the glory and the beauty of the
moonlight, to bathe in it, go mad in it, you said, "What! in
that slush in my slippers? Certainly not!" Now, that's what
I mean, Annabelle. [*He wanders to the window and looks out
at the moonlighted lawn.*] Oh, to think, to think! I might have
written another Moonlight Sonata!

ANNABELLE.

[*Folds up her sewing neatly and puts it in the work-basket, picks the stray threads off of her dress, brushes her skirts and folds her hands upon her stomach.*]

Hugh, we must separate!

HUGH.

Good Lord!

ANNABELLE.

We must. I see I've made a great mistake. I wish you had spoken of it sooner, but that can't be helped now. I never meant to make you waddle and cluck. I never meant to make your soul grow fat, I never did. I see now I'm a kind of a barnyard duck myself. I suppose you're growing like me and that is a very great pity. Hugh, I'm going home to mother.

HUGH.

But, Annabelle, you're crazy.

ANNABELLE.

Oh no, I'm not. I always intended to do the right thing by your Art, and I'll do it now.

HUGH.

But I don't want you to go home to your mother. I don't, indeed.

ANNABELLE.

Very likely not, just this minute. You'll feel the wrench a good deal, I dare say, but you'll be glad later because you'll be terribly uncomfortable and then you'll make perfectly beautiful music.

HUGH.

You don't mean you're going for good?

ANNABELLE.

Well, I don't want to spoil your career, do I? That's what you said just now, that your soul was dying because the dinner was hot—didn't you?

HUGH.

No!

ANNABELLE.

Oh—well, perhaps I misunderstood, but I'm sure it was something like that. Oh yes, I remember, you said your soul was getting fat. I'm awfully sorry.

HUGH.

Annabelle, look here! I never supposed you'd go off half-cock like this. I didn't indeed. I don't want you to go home to your mother. I just want you to—to come out in the moonlight and be romantic. [*He laughs foolishly and tries to take her hand.*] To feel the beauty and the romance and the joy. Can't you see what I mean?

ANNABELLE.

Now, Hugh, let us have a clear understanding.   You know
I'd do anything in the world for you, but oh please listen—if
I walked right out there in the wet in these slippers my feet
would feel so horrid I couldn't be romantic, I just couldn't.
Do be reasonable.   Can't you see what I mean?

HUGH.

[*Stalking to the window and back again.*]
Yes, I do see, and what I see is that you have no imagination.
You had better go home to your mother.   We are not mates.
Good-bye.   [*He goes out fiercely.*]
[ANNABELLE *opens her mouth as the curtain falls.*]

SCENE II: (*A year later.*) *A studio apartment in Greenwich Village in New York. It has attractive things in it, screens, embroideries, couch, but is most woefully untidy.*

Before, and as the curtain rises, HUGH *is playing the piano furiously. Arpeggios and runs dash from base to treble and back again. Chords crash like thunder. Triplets and ringlets and stream-lets tinkle about on top, then rush downwards to embrace the chords—a very tempestuoso glorioso of sound. He stops once or twice to jot down a note on a score. He gets up, rubs his stomach, and goes to some unwashed dishes on a table, the remains of afternoon tea, pokes among them unsuccessfully and then returns dolefully to the piano, first lighting a cigarette.* GLADYS *appears suddenly through the curtained doorway, back, and poses against the portières. She is tall and dark and angular and sinister, with a certain* BEAUTÉ DE DIABLE. *She is very smart and very decolleté, and she smokes a long, thin Italian cigar.* HUGH *looks up and sees her, and weaves into his theme passionate welcome. She smiles crookedly at him.*

HUGH.

My Beloved! [*He reaches out one hand, which she takes, leaning towards him.*]

GLADYS.

You call that—music?

HUGH.

Yes, I call that music.   Don't you?

GLADYS.

Would you mind telling me how much longer you expect to keep it up?

HUGH.

Until I get this idea down on paper.   Sorry you don't like it. It's my piano!   [*Bangs louder, then catches sight of her cigar.*] Throw that disgusting thing away!

GLADYS.

All right.
[*She does so, then takes his cigarette from his mouth and puts it in her own.*]
Ow wow!   What a noise!   [*Prinks before glass.*]   My ears!

HUGH.

[*Playing softly and beguilingly, and half chanting the question.*]
When do I get something to eat?

GLADYS.

[*Strolling around and stretching, dropping wrap on the floor.*]
I dunno.   I've had my supper.
    [*Fearful discords on piano.*]

HUGH.

    [*To the accompaniment of chords of jealous gloom.*]
You have?   With whom?

GLADYS.

Jim took me to the Ritz after the show.   What did you wait
for?   Guess you can scare up something somewhere if you try.
Isn't there some chocolate-cake over there?

[*She points to the tea-tray.   HUGH goes on playing—motif—
temper and hunger.*]

HUGH.

Chocolate-cake!   Ye gods!

[*Jealous-temper motif.   GLADYS unwinds herself luxuriously
onto the couch.*]

GLADYS.

Say, Hughie!

HUGH.

Yes?

[*Basso profundo.*]

GLADYS.

Did Old Grump take the Sonata?

HUGH.

No.

[*Anger motif.*]

GLADYS.

Thought not.   It's rot that sonata!   Little Hughie'll have
to try again.

[*Piano motif of temper and hunger plus wailing disappoint-
ment.*]

HUGH.

Woman! I'd like you to get me some supper, and get it
P. D. Q.
[*Masterful chord accompaniment on piano.*]

GLADYS.

[*Getting herself to sitting posture with astonishment.*]
Me! Why?

HUGH.

Why? Because I'm hungry, that's why—

GLADYS.

[*Cooingly.*]
How funny! Hughie! Has the Oriental gone to bed?

HUGH.

Probably—at two o'clock in the morning!
[*Piano begins to wail.*]

GLADYS.

No! Is it? And I've got to learn that part for eleven-
o'clock rehearsal tomorrow morning. Golly! Where 'd I put
it, anyhow? [*Searches about, making the general untidiness
worse. Finds MS. and curls herself up like a cat to study. Hunger
motif rises again on piano.*] Shut up, will you?

HUGH.

[*Playing more softly and looking up at her once or twice, opening his mouth as if to speak, then playing again, finally ending with a bang.*]

Why in thunder don't you get me my supper?
[*Seeing she isn't listening, he gets up and crosses to her. She glances up vaguely, but hardly hears, as she is absorbed in learning her lines.*] Please pay attention to me! Your little Hughie! Please!

GLADYS.

Oh Hugh, this is a lovely part! I'll be great in it—listen— [*Recites, then stumbles, then goes on mumbling the lines. HUGH takes the MS. out of her hands and casts it aside—then proceeds to make love to her.*]

HUGH.

Oh come on now, be a good fellow. There's a duck! Get me something to eat. You know how I love you. Please! [*He lays himself down by the low couch and puts his head in her lap, closes his eyes with a rapt smile, murmuring "Beloved." GLADYS twirls his hair in her fingers gracefully. He catches and kisses her fingers. Then, seeing his eyes are closed, she craftily reaches for her lines, while she continues petting him absent-mindedly with the free hand.*]

GLADYS.

Old Silly!

HUGH.

[*With his eyes closed.*]

Gladys, I'm very happy, very, very happy, but oh I'm so hungry! Don't let my love die of starvation. Don't! Won't you please get me some supper?

GLADYS.

In a minute! In a minute! This is so puzzling. [*Goes on murmuring lines and gesticulating. Finally she pats him so vaguely that she is patting his nose.*]

HUGH.

[*Opening his eyes.*]
Good God—what are you doing?

GLADYS.

Learning my part. I have to, don't I?

HUGH.

Learning your part! Ye gods! She's learning her part while I starve! Oh I'm so hungry! Hungry for love—hungry for my supper!
[*He dashes to the piano and plays starvation motif. Then there steals in the motif of passionate pain, begging, pleading, imploring. A wild medley follows, crescendo furioso. After a few ineffectual efforts to make him stop* GLADYS *puts down her MS. and listens judicially. Finally the music stops in some Dubussy chords. One seems to expect it to glide into another movement, but it doesn't.*]

GLADYS.

[*Regarding him with her head cocked and the cigarette bobbing from her lips.*]
Hughie! That hunger motif is perfectly great—it's one of the best things you do!

[From now on the relative action takes place in the same part of the stage as in preceding scene.]

HUGH.

[Leaving the piano.]

That's right! Make fun of my Art! Do you know what's the reason I can't play better, the reason Old Grump won't publish my stuff? Do you? Do you? [GLADYS *makes a queer little face at him.*] Well, I'll tell you the reason. It's you. Do you hear? It's you! You make me so damned uncomfortable I never get a chance to write decent music. It's all like that! I'm always hungry, I'm always cold, I never can find my clothes. When I want to be loved, when I need love, you go and study your part behind my back! I tell you it's killing me, just killing me!

GLADYS.

Are you serious?

HUGH.

Perfectly serious. My music is rotten—do you hear?—rotten! It's all alike—there's no contrast. If you knew anything about music you'd know you have to have different movements to make up a symphony, different moods. The calm of a sunset at sea—the stress of a great wind—dash of the waves against the rocks, then peace again—a shepherd's pipe in the gloaming— Well, when do I get a chance to compose a pastoral in this joint? It's nothing but rows and nasty cold meals and hurly-burly and chocolate-cake! I don't get sleep enough—my digestion is ruined—my socks have holes in them, bad holes— *[He kicks off his slippers and displays two toes bare.]*

GLADYS.

But, Hughie, you have me, think of that!

HUGH.

Yes, I know I have you, and I'm not likely to forget it!
As a first aid to a budding composer, you're a regular scream!
My soul is starving, I tell you, starving, and it's killing me,
killing me! [*He slumps gloomily onto the piano-stool.*]

GLADYS.

[*Rising majestically.*]

And what about me? I'd like to know where I get off? What
about my soul? A swell chance I've got to study my parts
with you banging that piano from morning till night! What
do you take me for, anyhow? A nice little Dickie-bird that's
got nothing to think about but your supper and your socks?
I've got my Art to think about—haven't I? Why, five minutes
ago, when you knew I just had to learn that part, you sat there
and banged on the piano on purpose and then you came and
dumped yourself down there! Who was uncomfortable then,
I'd like to know? And all you talked about was food! You're
always thinking about food, always complaining there isn't any.
Talking about your stomach when I'm learning my lines,
my great lines! You're so unromantic—Hugh— You are,
really!

[HUGH *looks startled. She has worked herself up to quite
a temper and now paces the room like an enraged
panther.*]

HUGH.

[After watching her.]

I see, I see it all.   I've made a terrible mistake.   We are both
IT, don't you see, and it won't work.   It will never work!

GLADYS.

What do you mean, Hugh?

HUGH.

*[Folds up his music, putting the scattered sheets in a neat pile,
arranges his hair and tie, then clasps his hands over his
stomach.]*

Gladys, we must separate.

GLADYS.

Good Lord!

HUGH.

I don't want to spoil your career.   I'm going home to Annabelle.

GLADYS.

[Making a panther spring.]

Never!   You're mine!

HUGH.

[Disengaging her hands.]

I see that I've done you a great wrong.   I always intended

to do the right thing by your Art, and I am going to do it now.
[*A puzzled, frightened look comes into his face as he speaks.*]

GLADYS.

[Clinging to him.]

Hughie, you're crazy. I don't want you to go home to Annabelle. I never supposed you'd go off half-cock like this. I
don't want you to go. I just want you to—to stop talking about
food while I'm studying my parts. It's a beautiful play, Hugh.
I die in the last act and I say such lovely things! You've no
idea what lovely things, and then you interrupt me talking
about supper when there's plenty of chocolate-cake right there!
If you'd just be a little more romantic, Hugh. Don't you see
what I mean?

[HUGH *looks still more frightened and puzzled. He clutches his
forehead.*]

HUGH.

[Gathering himself together.]

Now, Gladys, listen. Let us have a clear understanding.
You know I'd do anything in the world for you, but if I stopped
playing the piano while you learned your parts, and while you
slept, which is all morning long, why, there'd never be any time
to play at all. Do be reasonable. Don't you see what I mean?
[*At his own last words the frightened look comes into his face again.*]

GLADYS.

[*Who has stalked up stage and folded her arms while he has been
speaking.*]

Yes, I do see, and what I see is that you have no imagination.

You had better go home to Annabelle. We are not mates. Good-bye.

[HUGH *makes a wild clutch at his head with both hands and flees, presumably to* ANNABELLE. GLADYS *stands with her mouth open as the curtain falls.*]

CURTAIN.